DAY CARE DNA

HOW TO START, MAINTAIN, AND GROW A HEALTHY, VIBRANT CHILDREN'S DAY CARE

AARON BUTLER, JR.

authorHOUSE®

AuthorHouse™
1663 Liberty Drive
Bloomington, IN 47403
www.authorhouse.com
Phone: 1 (800) 839-8640

Published by AuthorHouse   04/12/2017

ISBN: 978-1-5246-8705-2 (sc)
ISBN: 978-1-5246-8703-8 (hc)
ISBN: 978-1-5246-8704-5 (e)

Library of Congress Control Number: 2017905279

Print information available on the last page.

To all the people who dare to fight past their give-up points and make their dreams come true. Someone said, "Don't go down a path already made but go where no one else has walked and leave a trail behind." This book is my trail behind.

CONTENTS

INTRODUCTION

When you are driving on your daily commute, have you ever noticed how many day cares or preschools you pass? I remember driving in a certain part of Orlando and literally seeing two to three day care centers per block. If you have children and pick them up from school, you've undoubtedly seen the many day care vans and minibuses in line picking up children for after-school care. So through observation, you might conclude that there's an oversaturation of childcare centers; but you would be gravely mistaken.

According to the US Census Bureau, in 2015, there were 23.9 million children between the ages of zero and five years old.[1] During that same period, ChildCare Aware of America reported that childcare providers care for approximately eleven million children younger than the age of five per week.[2] This doesn't even take into account the numbers of children needing before- and after-school care.

There is definitely a quantity need. Yet we also know there is a quality need as well. While great facilities, new vehicles, and the latest technology are all important aspects of the day care and preschool experience, there is something else that supersedes these elements and serves as the substratum for offering the best, and it's called *love*. Make no mistake. Children want to know how much you care before they learn how much you know. There is no substitute for genuine, unadulterated love.

This book is for

- the man or woman who has a burning desire to make a difference for kids through opening a childcare center but has no clue where to begin; and

- the provider who's established but struggling to be successful in enrollment, service, and profitability;

- the successful provider who already knows that, in order to stay successful, you need to be exposed to concepts and strategies that are working for others that you may not being doing so you can constantly grow and evolve.

In these pages, you will read about what works and what doesn't work when establishing and growing a healthy, thriving childcare center. You are getting full access to the good and bad of my first childcare center and the assurance that these are not just theories but tried and tested principles that work.

There is no doubt that I believe the strategies and information in this book will propel your existing center toward success or give you, as a new establishing provider, such an advantage that growth will overtake you. There is only so much that can be covered in this book, and that is why you can visit my website daycareman. com for additional information and services that will help you realize your dream.

I was asking some children one day what were their dreams. I got all kinds of responses from wanting to be an astronaut to be being the next Michael Jordan. Then one of the kids asked me "What's your dream?" I looked in their eyes and said, "My dream is to help you make your dreams come true."

I hope by writing this book I am able to help you make your dreams come true.

CHAPTER 1

HOW ARE YOU WIRED?

Entrepreneurship

Entrepreneurship is in my blood. I think it partially emulates from my father. My dad owned several different businesses and partnered in a few others, so his spirit in that regard may have rubbed off on me.

When I was in the sixth grade attending a parochial school in Michigan, I was a chubby child. Like most children, I loved candy and always had some on me. Everyday someone would say, "Aaron can I have some candy?" You must understand that, back then, vending machines were not in schools.

Being a fat kid, I admit I didn't like to share. (As I think about it now, I'm in super shape. I work out five days a week. And I still don't like to share my food. Maybe my weight had nothing to do with it.) Rather than giving my candy away, I came up with an idea. I used to buy my candy for a penny a piece. I bought a bunch of candy and started selling it for a dime a piece. What a margin! I was selling just to my own class and selling out every day. Then I decided to get a rep in every grade from fourth to ninth, and I was making bank!

I found a need, filled it, and made a profit! T. Harv Eker, in *Secrets of the Millionaire Mind*, said, "Do you know the definition of an entrepreneur? … A person who solves problems for people at a profit."[1]

I love to create! Making something from nothing and watching it grow gives me a thrill like nothing else. Some people think working for an employer is safe; but I don't view it that way. Employers can fire you at any time, so I've never understood this mentality. Safety to me is being able to create something where I can determine my own financial outcomes, and nobody can fire or lay me off.

I've been a protestant pastor for twenty-eight years. Don't worry. I'm not about to give you a sermon or pass an offering plate. The church I've pastored for the last eighteen years I literally started under a tree. I've heard pastors say they started in a storefront. Well I started in a no-front! We couldn't afford anything, and the tree was free. Within a week, we had a church building with a gymnasium. But that's another book. My point is, when working on anything, whether religious or secular, I've always been wired to create.

The all-important question is, "How are you wired?" At the end of the chapter I will give you some action points that will help you determine your wiring.

Leader or manager

When you are evaluating how you are wired, one of the important subquestions you will have to answer is, "Am I a leader or a manager?" I used to think that, if you were one, you were automatically the other. I was totally wrong. Leaders and managers have very different characteristics. Leaders are great at casting the vision. They can spell out the big picture and get everyone excited about the end result. Managers, on the other hand, are great at catching the vision and putting the skeleton together and then the flesh on the bones. Leaders are great at big picture. Managers are great at the details and the right now.

I am a leader. Can I manage? Yes, I can manage. When my business was small or when I lost a vital key position, I've stepped in and managed that division. Do I like managing? Absolutely not! Am I good at managing? No. I am very average at managing. However, when you are small in the beginning, a lot of times you have to do a bit of everything. As Tony Robbins said, "You are the cheapest employee you can hire, but it doesn't mean you are the best."

There are some people who advocate you need to spend time and work on strengthening your weaknesses. I couldn't disagree more. Time is a commodity that is being spent at a rapid rate and one you cannot redeem. Therefore, I believe in focusing on my strengths and hiring people to do what I am weak at or just plain don't like to do.

To franchise or not to franchise

There are some people who believe franchising is entrepreneurship and others who don't. I'll leave that for Paul Brown, who ignites this debate.[2] Yet it is very important for you to decide which path you choose to go down to achieve your childcare center dream.

4

Jeff Elgin wrote, "One of the misconceptions many people have is that franchise companies are looking for true entrepreneurs. Most franchise companies have a set plan that they have spent years of trial and error on and make their franchisers adhere to explicitly. If the truth be told most of us true entrepreneurs don't want to be told what to do."[3] Personally, I don't want to be told where I can advertise or that I can't implement a new idea I've come up with that I think would work in my market. So, franchising wasn't a good fit for me. In my opinion, franchising is more for those who are managers and are averse to large doses of risk.

ACTION STEPS

Answer the following questions:

    a. Do you structure your time well without someone else managing your schedule?

    b. Are you a disciplined person?

    c. Do you need a steady paycheck to feel safe, or do you enjoy working on commission?

    d. Is your desk messy or always organized?

    e. Do you find joy in making sure every detail is done to perfection?

    f. After conceptualizing, are you comfortable delegating and allowing others to evolve your ideas?

    g. Are you often accused of thinking months or years ahead of where you are at the time?

If you are self-motivated, well structured, disciplined, and don't need a steady paycheck to feel safe, then, you most likely have an entrepreneurial spirit.

If your desk is always neat and you thrive by paying attention to detail, you are most likely a manager.

Are you too busy for details? Is it about getting to the destination? If you are always accused of thinking beyond your means, these are usually signs you are a leader.

CHAPTER 2

DESIGNING THE DREAM

Imagination

I wonder if you were like me as a child. Did you have such a great imagination that you could pick up anything and transform it into reality with your mind? I was a huge *Star Trek* fan. Captain James Tiberius Kirk was the man! I would pick up a pear, and instantaneously it would become a communicator, and I would be hollering, "Scotty, get us out of here! Beam us up, Scotty!" You couldn't tell me that I wasn't the captain of the USS *Enterprise*.

I could go on and on, telling you stories of how I was Johnny Soko, and my wrist was the watch that made Giant Robot launch or my Lego was the device that turned me into Ultraman. My imagination gave me the freedom to be anyone I wanted to be and do anything I wanted to do.

Then something happened. I grew up. When I was a child, I was encouraged to dream, fantasize, and believe in the impossible. Yet the older I got, the more teachers and other adults discouraged me from dreaming. They told me to be practical and realistic. Thank God I didn't listen.

Your imagination is the greatest gift you have been blessed with to design your life. The mere fact you are reading this book means you already understand that the most successful people didn't achieve their success by being practical and realistic. Playing it safe will never give you the big returns you are looking for in life. I love the way T Harv Eker puts it. "I get ready, I fire, I aim!"[1] This is the exact opposite of what we've been taught—"ready, aim, fire!"

Most of the people in your life have consciously or unconsciously beaten down your imagination. More people sit around and try to top each other's stories on how hard life is, rather than try to top each other stories on how they are going to achieve their dreams. If you really want to succeed with your childcare center(s), you are going to have to learn how to dream again and hold on to that dream.

When you hold onto a dream, it becomes reality to you. Then you operate from that reality. Let me give a little bit of a crude but very relatable example. Do you remember being a child, asleep and dreaming that you were in the bathroom? In the dream, you went through all the motions. Then suddenly you felt something warm running down your leg and realized you were still in bed! Your subconscious didn't know the difference between reality and your dream. So, you operated as if you were in the bathroom.

If you can dream again and get that dream into your subconscious, you will start operating in life already from a position of "I can" rather than "I can't." That's a huge advantage, as it opens your vision to see opportunities and resources in front of you that normally you are blind to seeing. This is because your personal awareness system is enhanced.

When I decided to buy my black Lexus, something strange happened. I started seeing black Lexuses everywhere. Did they just suddenly appear? No, they didn't just appear out of nowhere. They were always there. The only difference was that my personal awareness system was heightened to notice black Lexuses because I had decided to buy a black Lexus.

Hotel in Birmingham, Alabama

In October 2006, I went to Birmingham, Alabama, to speak. This was an in state yearly engagement so I drove from Mobile. If you have ever driven I-65 on this route you know the most boring stretch of highway on God's green earth is between Mobile and Montgomery, Alabama.

However, this trip was different. As I was driving, I started thinking about whether I should open a day care. I had been toying with the idea for some time but seemed to always dismiss it for one reason or another. The person who had invited me to speak in Birmingham happened to have started a childcare center in the area, which had grown to almost four hundred children. This time, the thought just wouldn't leave me alone.

Due to a couple of conventions in the area, the hotel I always stayed in was booked, so I ended up in a hotel near the University of Alabama at Birmingham. I arrived at night, and the first thing I noticed was noise—lots and lots of noise! It was Saturday night, and kids were partying, and I had to be up at 6:00 a.m. I attempted to sleep, but the later it got, the louder the noise became.

Upset isn't an adequate adjective to describe how I was feeling. I couldn't sleep. I was tired of staring at the ceiling watching the fan spin, and I'm not a big TV watcher. I got up, went to the desk, and found the cheap pen and little notepad hotels provide in your room. I opened curtains, looked out at the square with all the partying kids, and sat down at the desk.

I started thinking, *If I had a daycare, what would it be like?* First, I sketched out buildings and floor plans. The property would be large enough to account for overflow space because, of course, my business would grow so fast I'd need it almost from day one of opening.

My spot near the window was getting too noisy, so I moved to the bar counter and started writing there. I wrote about how the children's faces would look coming in every day. I wrote about how some children would never want to leave and would beg to stay. I wrote down our own cartoon hero—Butlerman—and an area called little Aaron's Place.

In other words, I began to dream again as it pertained to opening a childcare center. I didn't consider how much anything would cost or if I had the expertise to do any of the work. I simply dreamed. It's amazing what happens when you dream and take off the weights of "what if" or "how will" or "how much." The freedom you get from the experience of dreaming and imagination is simply amazing.

It's not what you know; it's who you know

In all honesty, the dreams I started fully having in that hotel room—or as a matter of fact, most of the dreams I've ever had—would have never come true if it had not been for the people I knew. I have been blessed to have elders and friends in my life who were dreamers and achievers. The quickest way to kill a dreamer and his or her dream is to put him or her around a group of people who have given into mediocrity and are driven by circumstance.

Just the other day, while I was writing this book, a friend of mine called me and told me he was going to make a million dollars in ninety days. He told me how he was going to do it and that he might write a book about how he did it.

My response? I gave him a couple of additional ideas to go along with his process that might help him achieve his goal. Now, have I ever made a million dollars in ninety days? No not yet, I have not. However, I have started corporations that have made over a million dollars over a longer period. Just because I haven't done it in ninety days doesn't mean it's not possible. There are plenty of people who have, and even if there weren't, my friend could be the first!

Our only limits are the ones we put on ourselves. My friend called me because he knew he would not get a "you can't do that" response. It's not that I'm a yes-man. Everyone who knows me knows you don't ask my opinion if you can't handle a straightforward response. However, I am of the school of Captain James T. Kirk. Kirk was the only person to pass Starfleet Academy's final test simulation. How did he do it? He reprogramed the simulation. Kirk's philosophy was that there's always a way to win.

I cannot emphasize enough the need for you to have dreamers/ achievers in your life. You need to be around other people who think big so their infectious spirit of optimism and possibility will constantly rub off on you.

Let's face it. Most people are negative. It's not that they see the glass half empty, instead of half full. They don't even see a glass because they believe somebody took their glass. That's why they can't get ahead. When you associate with these kinds of people, don't make the foolish mistake of thinking sharing your dream is going to inspire them. More than likely, their negative response is going to depress you! This does not just go for friends. It includes family as well. You must make a conscious effort to cut all contact with people who aren't possibility thinkers. In the case of family, you should limit contact with those who are in the realm of the unbelievers in dreams coming true.

If you are married, it is imperative that your spouse be on board. I remember twenty years ago coming home to my wife at the time and sharing an idea I had to expand a business I was running in a certain department. The first thing out of her mouth was, "What makes you think you can do that?"

I was livid but didn't say a word. Two things I swore to myself. First, I'd never share another idea I had with her again. Second, I was not only going to do it, I was going to do it in half the time and shove it in her face!

I achieved both objectives. Suffice to say, she is my ex-wife.

To be fair, over the years, she has said I was the only person she ever met who spoke a dream and made it happen. She even went so far as to say that she wished she was like me in that regard.

People telling me I can't do something has always been an extreme motivator for me. But most people are not wired that way. When a significant other throws water on a dream that's on fire, most people let him or her put the fire out without a fight. I can only speak for me, but I would not dare marry someone who was negative. Been there, done that. I am not going back!

You will note, I wrote earlier *dreamers/achievers*. It's not enough to associate with dreamers. You need to associate with dreamers who turn their dreams into reality. Many people have dreams or ideas. How many people make them come to pass? You need friends who buck the odds, go against the grain, and are not the norm. Normal behavior doesn't achieve extraordinary results. Thomas Edison, with only twelve weeks of formal education, was thought of to be "not normal" until, after thousands of attempts, he made the lightbulb.[2] Then he was thought of as a genius! Don't be afraid to associate with out-of-the-box thinkers because, guess what? You are one of those out-of-the-box thinkers, or you wouldn't be reading this book.

Show me how

You need a mentor. Yes, you need a mentor! I'm repeating myself because this is vitally important. Having a mentor and having dreamers/achievers in your life is far more important than the information you may or may not know about the business.

I can hear some of you saying, "Well I'm cooked then because I don't know anyone in the business to mentor me." You are wrong. You know me. Through these pages, you know me, and I will show you how to get a direct mentor you may already know or a distant mentor later. Plus, you can contact me at daycareman.com, and my team can provide you mentorship. So don't sweat it. The key is realizing you need one.

I remembering listening to a recording back in the '80s of Rick Warren, author of the best seller *The Purpose Driven Life*. "It's good to learn from your mistakes," he says, "but it's better to learn from someone else's mistakes." Tony Robbins says the way he achieves maximum success and cuts decades into days is by modeling. He finds the best model and studies it.

As I am writing this book, I'm in the process of trying to find a mentor as we prepare to open centers in multiple states at the same time. You will always need a mentor at every level. What a mentor will pour into your life is priceless.

I was tremendously blessed to have my best friend as my first day care mentor. Although my father had a day care, I was so young at the time that I didn't remember the operation. I remember going to my friend's day care and him giving me all access. I walked in classrooms, talked to staff, and saw vital papers and statistics. I learned the philosophy behind the center. Most important, they shared what mistakes they'd made. This gave me a huge advantage.

That's what mentorship does—gives you a huge advantage. Let's face it that's what you need if you are going to win an advantage at the game of childcare. Before someone takes offense at the term "game," that is how I look at life—as a game. I'm extremely competitive, so whenever I play a game I only play to win. Almost every conceivable question I had, my friend answered.

Sometimes, though, the answers were, "I don't know." I'd ask unreasonable questions like, "How long will it take me to get to a hundred children?" He could only respond, "Aaron, it took us this amount of time. I'm not sure how long it will take you."

As I've stated, I have a whole company that is dedicated to your success as a childcare provider, and it can be contacted at daycareman.com. We have an outstanding team ready to mentor you in every facet and even willing to do some of the work for you if you'd like. Yet here are some ideas on how to find and approach a potential mentor:

- *Look for the top childcare providers in your state or region* – Call the owner or the director and say how much you admire the center's excellence in childcare and that you'd like to take him or her to lunch at some nice expensive restaurant just to pick his or her brain for thirty minutes.

- *Read books and articles and view YouTube videos on successful childcare centers and corporations* – Sometimes you may not be able to reach the CEO or director. Or due to their distance, you can't travel to them. Reading every article you can find or viewing every interview on YouTube is a form of indirect mentorship that can prove to be invaluable.

- *Locate successful retired providers and directors* – Everyone loves to tell old "war stories" of how they went through this adversity or that adversity and came out on the winning side. You can gain so much insight and knowledge through their successes and failures. Again, offer to take them to a very nice restaurant. As a matter of fact, let them pick.

There is no sense in reinventing the wheel. Mentors will save you time and money and accelerate your ability to make money much faster.

Finding your voice

Right now, you need to decide to whom you want to provide childcare services. I know you may want to provide services to all children, no matter socioeconomics or demographics, but it rarely works out that way. It is true; "birds of a feather flock together." When is the last time you saw a billionaire living in the ghetto? Or when is the last time you saw someone on welfare living in One57 in New York. Likeminded people tend to congregate and commune together.

You should decide what type of parent you want to offer your services to. Yes, you can serve multiple types, but for the most part, that will mean having multiple centers in different parts of town that cater to different kinds of people. I am going to give you a brief overview of the types of communities you can serve, as well as the different types of centers you can choose to be.

Communities:

- *Low-income, subsidized families* – This community consists primarily of families who are either below the poverty line or whose incomes are low enough that the government will financially compensate you for all or part of the care. It is important for you to know that the state reimbursement program, which is tied to the federal government, is separate from the county program, which can reimburse you as well. These are two different money pots, and thus, funds are distributed differently.

o   Pros of the state program:

1. Most states pay you weekly through direct deposit. In the past, you were paid once a month by check through the mail, which could be a nightmare if your forty thousand-dollar check was lost or mailed late and you had obligations to meet.

2. You know exactly how much money is coming a week in advance and can file your payment dispute adjustment forms quickly and be reimbursed within thirty days.

3. You are notified weeks in advance if a child is about to be dropped from the program. This gives you time to fill that spot without a lot of gap in income.

4. Parents in general tend not to give you many problems. They primarily just want to know their children are safe and being loved.

o   Pros of the county program:

1. None, absolutely none, from a provider standpoint. I do not accept children who are funded by the county.

○ Cons of the state program:

1. The state sets the ceiling on what it will pay per child for care. Often it is well-below-market price. You can charge more, but the subsidized parents must make up the difference, and if they can barely pay the copay, how are they going to pay an additional fifty dollars per week just to keep up with market pricing?

   (The copay is the amount the parent must pay along with the subsidy to meet the cost of the childcare. Most copays are between four and ten dollars per week. They are based off income.

2. You cannot charge a private paying parent a different rate than you charge a subsidized parent. All rates must be the same.

3. Some states have the card-swiping Time and Attendance program, and it can be a nightmare getting parents to swipe and stay current with their

swiping so you are paid on time and accurately. If you have centers in Alabama or North Carolina as I do you, know from personal experience what I'm writing about.

4. Most parents are not as engaged and concerned with a curriculum. They are lackluster as it relates to a preschool education for their children.

o   Cons of the county program:

1. In my experience, I've had the county pay me as late as six months after service was rendered. Therefore, I do not accept children who are subsidized by the county.

2. The county program is a bridge for the client while he or she is getting transferred to the state. In-program communication between staffers, even those who may simply be on two different floors, can take weeks, and you'll be left waiting because of inefficiency.

- *Private-pay, middle-class families* – I am grouping these people as one. There are actually three segments to this group—lower middle class, middle class, and upper middle class.

o   Pros:

1. There is no middleman to receive payment from. You are paid in full, directly by the parents themselves.

2. If you are more of an educationally based program in general, parents tend to be more supportive of your curriculum objectives.

3. You can set your tuition as high as you want without a preset ceiling by the government.

o   Cons

1. If these parents have a financial crisis, usually one of the first things they cut is childcare—often without giving you the minimum two-week notice you should require in your parent handbook. This was evidenced greatly in the state of Georgia during the Great Recession, and inventory of buildings is still plenteous because it hasn't fully recovered.[3]

2. These parents tend to be more particular about every little thing. I don't blame them. They are paying hundreds of dollars per week for their most

precious assets—their children—to be cared for. However, you need to be ready because some parents are unreasonable, and it can be very aggravating to say the least.

- Ethnicities
  - Ethnic tendencies play a vital part in determining who you will offer your services to. If you are one of these politically correct, must-be-racially sensitive-to-the-infinite-degree people, get over it! You want to be successful, and you need an edge.
  - Statistics show that African Americans put their children in childcare the most. Caucasians follow in second place, while Hispanics are the least likely to place their children in day care.[4] While there are universal things that appeal to all ethnicities, such as cleanliness, there are distinct things that are unique to cultures that you need to be aware of.
    1. Here's an example. An African American opens a center in Orlando, Florida. Will Hispanics be willing to place their children in that center? The answer is yes and no. Hispanics encompass several

Latino communities. Puerto Ricans, in general, would be much more willing to place their children in that center than would Argentinians.

2. You must be cognizant in a community of who gets along with whom.

o It's also imperative that you are aware of the needs of the various communities as they relate to childcare services. Their individual needs will affect the services you offer and may be the edge you need to be the number one provider in your area.

- Services

   o What kind of childcare services are you going to offer?

   1. Infant care only

   2. Infant to five years old

   3. Infant to twelve years old

   4. Before-school care

   5. After-school care

   6. Transportation between your center and school for your before- and after-schoolers.

   7. Transportation between home and your center.

   8. Tutoring

9. All of the above

o   You must decide what you are going to offer because it effects how you lay the foundation for your center. For example, transportation will require you to purchase or lease buses. Those buses will need drivers and riders. More equipment and more staff will be needed on the front end.

o   In chapter 6, "Financial Basics," I go into more detail about start-up capital.

ACTION STEPS

1. Get a pen and some paper and begin to write out the kind of day care center you want to create. Don't worry about how much it will cost or your current skill level. Just dream! Be as specific as possible.

2. Identify the dreamers/achievers in your life right now. Make a conscious effort to hang around them and talk about what they are doing in their lives. This will motivate you to achieve your dream.

3. Find a mentor. Look for a model that is the closest to what you want to create. Contact the owner or corporate head.

Follow the suggestions in the chapter. And remember, don't be cheap!

4. Decide what type of community you want to specialize in serving. Remember you can't be all things to all people.

CHAPTER 3

IT'S TRUE: LOCATION, LOCATION, LOCATION!

Accessibility matters

When you are picking a location for your day care, the first and foremost question you must ask yourself is, "How accessible is my location?"

When answering this, you may immediately think you want a center on a busy highway with a lot of traffic. That is not necessarily true for several reasons. For example, I know a day care that is located on a major highway. From 7:15 to 9:00 a.m., it is bumper-to-bumper traffic. How easy do you think it is for that center's parents to drive in and out of the property?

You need to establish your location criteria. Have you ever noticed that Walgreen's only builds stores on corners? Do you think that is coincidental? No. It's a part of their location criteria for new stores.[1] My location criteria are:

1. It must be within five minutes of a major interstate.

2. It must be within two minutes of a major highway.

3. It must be on a street adjacent to that major highway.

4. It must have a minimum of six feeder schools in a five-minute radius from my location.

Because I do before- and after-school care, number four is paramount for me to be successful.

Property

The lay of the land on which you will house your childcare center needs to be congruent with the building and space requirements you will need.

A few months back, I was considering purchasing a day care center that had shut down for an additional location. While the location met my criteria and the building was doable, the property was not. This was an old chain day care building. If you are familiar with these, all of them have one thing in common—a small singular parking lot in the front of the building. This building was licensed for two hundred kids but only had eight parking spaces. Now, a center of mine will have six buses. Where would the staff or parents park? With only one entrance in the front, that was going to be a logistical nightmare.

I prefer an acre and a half to two acres of property. That will allow you to do my horseshoe flow plan and ensures there are never any traffic jams or parent backups. This gives you plenty of room for your buses in the back or front and gives you space for your playground. Plus, it gives you expansion space.

Building

Whether you are purchasing an existing day care building, remodeling a building into a day care facility, or building from the ground up, you do not want a building smaller than eight thousand square feet. When you start going below this size, you affect your ability to be profitable. The idea is not for you to work in the center. I understand that, in the beginning, you have to, but the goal is for you to focus on creating new centers while you have an excellent staff to run your centers. If you go below that size, you will make it necessary for you to work in the center just to get a paycheck. So understand, size matters!

Let's say you have that eight thousand-square foot building. We are going to take away three thousand square feet for hallways, foyer, mechanical room, kitchen, and offices, so you have five thousand square feet left to work. If you have twenty kids in a classroom and the minimum square footage is thirty-five square feet per child, each classroom is going to be seven hundred square feet. (Please note that the minimum footage per child varies per county and state. Contact us at daycareman.com for current stats.)

At seven hundred square feet apiece, your building can have seven classrooms with a total of 140 children at a time. Now you use the number 140 to help determine your overall operating budget. I will go over that in the chapter on finance. To give you a quick idea, if you have 140 kids and you have an average weekly tuition of $125 per child, your yearly gross will be $910,000. Keep in mind, that's operating at full capacity. You want to design your profitability plan so you don't have to be at 100 percent capacity to be profitable. I hope you can see how the size of your building is key to your success.

I know of a person who bought a building in an excellent location with plans to have over two hundred full-time children.

When the Department of Human Resources, the health department, and the fire department inspected, they all denied the owner the right to open a day care. Why? Because of the design of the building. The owner planned on opening the day care on the second floor. In most areas, that's an absolute no from the beginning. The only exception is sometimes they will allow you to have school-age children on a second floor.

Then there was a church not far from one of my centers that built a new church, which cost over $2 million. The church opened a day care in the new building. When officials heard, they came out and shut the day care down. Now this church had a day care in its previous building. What that pastor and leadership team didn't realize was that religious facilities were grandfathered if they had existing facilities. However, if you build a brand-new facility, you must submit the plans to DHR, the health department, the fire marshal, and building inspector. They must be cognizant of what spaces will be used for childcare. Those spaces must conform to building regulations for a childcare facility.

If either of these would-be day care owners had consulted with my team, they would have saved hundreds of thousands of dollars.

There are so many things to consider with the classrooms beyond furniture and bulletin boards. Most authorities require a dump sink, wash sink, and splash guards. If a sprinkler system is not installed, there must be outside access from that room. Floors must be finished in a certain way. Doors should be fire rated, with automatic adjustable closers. Some authorities allow regular-size sinks and commodes with steps; however, I always use child-size and leveled sinks and commodes.

The previously mentioned details are just a few of the things that should be considered when choosing a building. Please do not consider this an exhaustive list.

ACTION STEPS

1. Determine your location criteria.
2. Be sure to keep in mind what services you will offer.
3. Make sure the land is large enough.
4. Have plenty of parking.
5. Make sure you can establish an easy traffic flow plan that will not cause congestion.
6. Be sure your building is a minimum of eight thousand square feet.

7. Get someone who knows all the codes and ordinances for every department that must inspect your property. You can contact us at daycareman.com. We know the regulations for all states and territories.

CHAPTER 4

BUILD A GREAT TEAM

Don't do it alone

One of the common feelings when starting or operating an entrepreneurial venture is that you are alone. You feel like nobody cares more about your business than you do. In a lot of cases, you are right. However, if you can develop a system where people take ownership of the business through a feeling of unity and belonging to something greater than themselves, then you are on the verge of developing people who care as much as you do.

I must admit I have always been a one-man show for the most part. I think I had this implanted in my subconscious by watching my mother when I was a child. She would make these beautiful posters for her church by hand by herself. My mother is old-school.

She graduated valedictorian of her undergraduate class at Jackson State University in Jackson, Mississippi. She graduated as one of the top students in her graduate studies at Bradley University in Peoria, Illinois. She's a retired elementary teacher in her late seventies now, who doesn't use stencils. She cuts letters free hand and writes beautifully. I mention all this because, regardless of arthritis, she still gets in the middle of the floor now and makes the most beautiful posters—alone.

I remember asking her once why she didn't let people help her, and her reply was, "If you want something done right, you have to do it yourself."

There were times she allowed her sister to help her. Yes, she was a retired schoolteacher as well, but she was the only person my mom ever let help her.

While I know, my mom thought she was teaching me a good lesson, she was reinforcing the biggest mistake we entrepreneurs make in business: "It's me against the world."

Okay while that sounds good, let's really look at that statement. Per the United Nations in 2016, there are an estimated 7.4 billion people on this planet—7.4 billion people![1] Do you really think you can beat 7.4 billion in a fight? Hell, Dwayne "The Rock" Johnson couldn't Rock Bottom or People's Elbow 7.4 billion people. My point is you don't want to be against the world. You want to get the world to work for you.

In the early days, I did everything. I was the cook, van driver, classroom teacher, janitor, payroll specialist—you name it; I did it. I used to go home after working fourteen hours and fall asleep at the dinner table. My youngest son would simply turn the light off. That's right. That little joker wasn't kind enough to wake me up and tell me to go to bed! To his credit, he saw how hard I was working and gave up football in high school one year to help me get that center off the ground. So, I understand doing everything in the beginning. But even then, you are not doing everything. I believe God—you may say the universe—sends people along to help you because, at some point in your life, you sowed the seed by helping someone else. You probably don't even remember the many people you've helped.

Besides my best friend, Dr. Karnie C. Smith, who I've referenced already, there was one person God sent into my life for a season. Frankly, without her, I would not be writing this book because there would be nothing to write about. Shirley is now married and is called Mrs. Shirley. She was an area leader and daycare teacher at a government childcare facility. She set up my menus, trained my teachers, organized my classrooms, did my lesson plans, and even drove every week one hour to help me do my shopping.

At that time, my team was Karnie, Shirley, and myself. My point is, you always have a team, whether you realize it or not. The objective is to make the team bigger and for you not to become the bottleneck stopping the flow.

Team summary

Below, I am going to list members of my team. Some of the people mentioned you might not think of as team members. Keep an open mind because this has been critical to my success. By the way, this team is expanding more and more every day.

Lawyers

The two primary law firms I employ are in Mobile, Alabama, and Birmingham, Alabama. My primary lawyer, Mark, has represented me for almost twenty years. He is the chief partner of his law firm and has proved invaluable, to say the least.

You need lawyers who have expertise in specific areas. For example, with property, Mark doesn't handle that; he refers me to Mike, one of the other partners in the firm. When you are starting your corporation, you want a lawyer whose expertise is in corporations. Don't get a lawyer who will charge you an arm and a leg and use LegalZoom because he or she only knows a little more about that area of law than you do.

Once you find a good lawyer, keep a good relationship with him or her. Your lawyer's advice will be valuable, and after twenty years, he or she won't charge you for every phone call.

Bankers

I know there are those of you who look at banks as adversaries. I totally understand why. I have had some not so good experiences with banks. One bank I paid off five loans to and the current one hadn't been late, and they tried to jump our interest rate and cut us from a five-year balloon, fifteen-year amortization to a two-year balloon. What was so despicable was that, the night before, the banker and I had gone over the five-year terms. The next day, he was too scared to stay in the conference room while I signed the papers. He had his female assistant try to bully me. My treasurer was in the room. We'll just say I tore the papers up in their face and told them to …well young people may be reading. I write all that to demonstrate that I understand.

Because of my philosophy of maintaining good business relationships, I have a banker I've had a relationship with for over twenty years. While I have more than one good banking relationship, there is one banker who is the absolute best—Carla. Carla has done great business deals for me, and most of the time, I never even step into her office. She has navigated things I needed done with style, grace, and expertise like I've never seen. Get a great banker!

Insurance brokers

In the beginning, I use to only go to one provider. About seven years ago, I changed that and started going to an insurance broker. My guy, Chris, can write for any of the major companies and often gets me much better rates than I'd get if I just went to one firm. My needs vary with different business entities, so this works best for me.

Always—I repeat, always—have insurance for anything you can't write a check and cover out of your pocket.

Accountants

I've only had two accounting firms in twenty plus years. Again, this goes to establishing and maintaining relationships. I recommend you only use certified public accountants. When banks and other financial institutions want your financials certified, you will need a CPA. Yes, there are accountants who are not certified, but only use CPAs. It will save you time and headaches.

Payroll

The greatest thing I ever found was the payroll company I outsource to. I love it and have used them for years. Outsource your payroll to a good payroll company. They will be up to date with all the IRS changes and save you a lot of time and headaches as well.

Architect

Your architect will be one of your first team members picked and one of the most vital. You want to choose the best certified and most credentialed architect. This is the person who will draft your floor plan; place his or her stamp on it; and submit it to the building, fire, health, and human resources/services departments. A competent architect will know the codes and regulations for your projects and will help eliminate you doing unnecessary things that aren't a part of the code.

One word of advice—never trust the numbers an architect gives you. Only go off the bids of your building contractor. I've had architects' numbers be off by as much as 50 percent.

Building contractor

Only use licensed and bonded contractors. The contractors I use have been referred to me by experts in the field who have used these individuals. Now that I've worked with them myself, I know, from experience they do quality work. However, research and read several—and I mean several—reviews by people on various social media lists. You don't need the biggest contractor in town if you are just renovating or remodeling a building. The size and scope of the job will determine if you need a general contractor or specialized subcontractors.

Chief maintenance director

I am blessed beyond measure to have one of the most talented maintenance director's in the country. Harold has been with me for over twenty years. He is the maintenance director for our county Head Start program as well. His knowledge of all the ordinances, requirements, and inspectors was and is priceless. He has saved me thousands of dollars and is worth his weight in gold.

Radio

I will cover radio in more detail in chapter 8, "Brag Please." In brief, I advertise on the largest station in whatever market I have a center. My dad taught me to never deal with the representative; always go to the boss.

Others

I consider my service representatives at Chevy and Ford a part of my team. I've picked up the phone many times and told them I had to have a vehicle fixed in two hours, and they have made it happen.

The plumbing and electrical companies I use I consider a part of my team, as well as my web designer, sound engineers Dennis, Barry, Wilma and my day care software cloud provider.

Day care staff

When it comes to your childcare staff, experience in actual childcare matters. Just because someone is an elementary school teacher doesn't mean he or she can walk in and be a director of a center. I made this crucial mistake in my early days. You want somebody who knows the job. There is no substitute for experience. Middle-age and up staff members have, on a percentage basis, worked out far better for me than millennials. I do have a few outstanding millennials who work for me. But honestly, they have been few and far in-between. Work ethic differences between generations are real.

Jim Collins, in *Good to Great: Why Some Companies Make the Leap …and Others Don't*, noted that one of the most important things you must do in order for a business to be successful is "get the right people on the bus."[2] He means that you want to hire the best-qualified person you can at the time for any given position. Remember you don't just want someone who can do the job you want someone who is the best fit for the job. You want these people for the long haul because, although prevalent in this business, you want to cut your employee turnover rate as much as possible.

Our staff positions include site director, director of transportation, director of curriculum, lead teacher, teachers, assistant teachers, drivers, riders, nurse, kitchen staff, maintenance and office staff.

It is important to note that you cannot just hire anyone to work in a childcare facility. Every state has specific requirements that must be met in order for a person to be qualified to work in a day care center. You can contact us at daycareman.com for those specific requirements in your area.

More than you thought

After reading all this, if you are a novice, you may be feeling somewhat overwhelmed about the scope of the team you will need. As a matter of fact, all the information you have read so far may be causing you to have second thoughts, and the book isn't even finished. This is what Seth Godin calls "the Dip"—the great chasm between where you are when you start thinking about entering a venture and doing the venture. Godin proposes every industry has that dip to weed out the weak and uncommitted and keep them from entering the field.[3]

I remember a lady who was starting a day care at the same time I was starting a center. She had spent over $100,000 and, after a year, still was not open. She called me and told me one day, "I can't do this anymore. I quit. Are you going to keep going through all this mess?"

I responded, "I can't quit. I'm too far along. Failure isn't an option because I have no bridge to go back on."

That's the attitude you must have—you must believe that *failure is not an option*. I have a quote hanging in my office by Napoleon Bonaparte, which reads, "Impossible is a word to be found only in the dictionary of fools." I truly believe nothing is impossible if you have a strong enough "why" for achieving it. When you determine that obstacles are nothing but commas in the sentence of life and not periods, you will see the word *impossible* disappear out of your life.

Your advantage

The great advantage you have is that you don't have to go through the dip alone. You have me and my team, and we'll walk with you along every step of the way until you can walk on your own. Due to this advantage, success is your only option now.

ACTION STEPS

1. Start identifying your team right now. Use this chapter as a guide.

2. Determine who you will need to add to your team so you can get started.

3. Develop a plan for attracting the best people to work for you.

CHAPTER 5

FINDING YOUR NICHE

Circumstances not on my side

It was 2008 at the height of the Great Recession. Here I was, opening a day care. Who opens a day care in the middle of a recession? See the hand going up over in the corner? It's mine. I remember a member of the church I pastored telling me it would make more sense for me to fix the holes in the parking lot than to open a day care center.

Many people felt that person's comment was a valid one. At the time, there were approximately fifteen day cares open, all within five minutes from my location. There was a church with a huge building located across the street that had a day care and a gymnasium! Yes, a full-fledged gymnasium, which was awesome at the time. Now keep in mind all I had to operate was an eight thousand-square foot building, compared to a twenty thousand plus-square foot building across the street. To make matters worse, I didn't even have a playground. (To this day that center doesn't have a playground.) All the odds said this would be another new business failure. It looked like this day care was going to end up in the new business graveyard. At least that was the vantage point of everyone except me.

It's not arrogance; it's confidence

I remember someone remarked to me, "All these day cares have the best of everything, and you don't even have a playground or a bus."

I replied, "They don't have everything."

The gentleman asked, "What are they missing?"

I said, "They don't have me!"

The gentleman laughed and said, "That's very arrogant of you."

I stated, "It's not arrogance. It's confidence."

What this gentleman didn't know was my story. He didn't know I had been on my own since I was sixteen when my father committed suicide. He didn't know I had been homeless. He didn't know I had started a church literally under a tree. He didn't know my story. This was nothing compared to the things I'd been through in my life but another opportunity. Notice I said *opportunity*, not *problem*. I believe every "problem," as it were, is nothing but an opportunity to grow. Once you solve that problem, it's never a problem again; it's now an answer.

What's in your house?

The gentleman was right, to a degree. Seemingly every day care had more resources than me. I didn't have a playground. I didn't have a bus. To make matters worse, I was broke. Cost estimates by my architect were way off, and the little surplus money I had disappeared quicker than a woman in a David Copperfield show in Las Vegas.

Some of you are probably thinking, *Why didn't you build a playground?* I had a portion of our property behind the back parking lot cleared for a playground. Unbeknownst to me at the time, a playground must be adjacent to the building. So, I spent the money to clear the land but couldn't put in a playground. Based on how I had my traffic flow, I didn't see at the time where I could locate the playground adjacent to the building. Another tidbit of information that makes this book well worth the price you paid.

Despite being out-resourced, I was determined not to be beaten. Catch this truth: If you have a strong enough desire, nothing—I repeat, nothing—can stop you. You may be thinking, *Aaron, a lack of resources was stopping you*. No, as Tony Robbins said in one of his Business Mastery seminars, "A lack of resources is never the problem. The problem is you not being resourceful enough to find the resources."

This being the case, the first thing I asked myself was, "What's in my house?" In other words, what resources do I have at my disposal? When I took inventory, I realized the best resource I had above my competition was my desire to exceed my parents' expectations. This realization opened a new question. Can I beat my competition at their game? The answer was no.

Can't win the game? Be a game changer

I realistically looked at how the game was being played and the number of participants and realized I couldn't beat them playing per their rules. The good thing was that I realized this after I had already started competing. I am such a competitor there was no way I would give up since I had already started. If I'd had this mind-set prior to starting, you probably wouldn't be reading this book because I would not have even entered the game.

I started evaluating what my clientele's biggest problem was. The answer was so close in front of me that it could have slapped my face. Very few of my parents had dependable transportation. While most day cares took children to school and picked them up from school, nobody was picking kids up from home and taking them back home. Further, nobody did it for free! Day cares were charging as much as much as forty dollars per week for van/bus service to and from school. Now, parents in the area had a hard enough time paying the four- to ten-dollar co-pay per child per week. Adding an additional forty dollars for transportation, for many families, was killing them financially. What if I offered free transportation to and from home?

Until this point, I was using my car as transportation to drop kids off and pick them up from school. To pull this off meant I had to make an investment in a van. Three problems jumped up immediately in my face. First, I was broke. Second, my credit was maxed out. Third, I didn't have enough kids to fill a van up.

Here is where I learned a huge lesson. You don't buy something for your business *after* you need it. You buy it *before* you need it. I made the calculated risk and bought a van. I never take risks. I always take calculated risks. There is a difference. Paul B. Brown wrote, "Risk takers risk it all and leave a lot up to chance. Calculated risk taker take small steps and try to mitigate more and more risk with each step they take."[1] I determined that, if I bought the van and I wasn't successful, I could always sell the vehicle and remain in business.

Since, at the time, I had neither the money nor the credit to buy the vehicle, I had to find someone who would sign for it, and I would pay the note. I was blessed to have someone who has always believed in me and seen me always produce. I found a great deal on a van in Georgia, and Barbara signed for it.

I remember driving that van back from Georgia and thinking, *I don't even have enough of an enrollment to fill this van right now.* What I didn't realize was that, if I'd had enough to fill up that van, then I wouldn't have had any room for growth. Again, you don't buy equipment when you need it. You buy it before you need it!

The next day I made up flyers and printed on them "Free Transportation—we'll pick your children up from home and bring them back free of charge anywhere in the metro area."

Thirty days later, not only was that van full; I needed another one.

I realized I had to introduce a game changer, not only to get a competitive edge but also to be completely unique. I'm the *only* one who offers this service to the whole metro area free of charge. I've learned—don't try to beat your competition at what they do best. Beat them by doing what they *are not* doing at the highest level possible.

ACTION STEPS

1. Look in the mirror and ask yourself, "Do I believe in the person I am looking at?"

   a. If the answer is a genuine yes, then move on to the next step.

   b. If the answer is no, start identifying the areas where you lack confidence and address them. There are several books and programs that can help you.

2. Identify what you bring to the table that no one else does.

3. Come up with a game-changing idea no one else is doing.

CHAPTER 6

FINANCIAL BASICS

First order, make a profit

Bob Proctor once said, "The first order of business is to make a profit. The purpose of an organization is to make life more meaningful."

Like you, I am very passionate about the welfare of children. You may have a heart for special-needs children, low-income children, at-risk children, or children in general. Yes, our objective is to make a difference. But the fact is, you can't make a major difference without money. I'm a firm believer in prayer; however, none of my prayers have ever paid for chemotherapy for a child facing cancer.

You must not get caught up in the current world trend that suggests making money is bad. You cannot afford to give in to the ignorance of people who think having excess means you are greedy or are hindering someone else from obtaining wealth. The fact of the matter is, there is no shortage of money. Governments keep printing the stuff every day. There is a shortage of people who have an idea, turn it into a magnificent obsession, and bring it into fruition.

Think about it. Can you do more good in the world making $50 million a year versus making $50,000 a year? How many people could you feed or cancer treatments could you pay for in a year if you gave away just 10 percent of your income—at $50 million a year? What if you got radical and gave away 90 percent of your income and lived off 10 percent? That $45 million a year could make a world of difference, and I could live off $5 million a year with no problem; I don't know about you.

If you don't have a wealth mentality you must develop one if you are going to be successful. Your childcare business is *not* a charity. If you don't make a profit, you will not be in business long, and you will not be making a difference in the lives of children through childcare.

This chapter is on money basics in childcare. By no means is this an exhaustive treatise on finance as it pertains to your childcare center. I am just mentioning a few concise things to prime your thinking in this regard. You should always consult with financial experts for planning and implementation.

Start-up costs

The number one question I am asked, in regards to childcare, is how much does it cost to start a day care? My answer is always, "It depends." There are so many forms of childcare your particular center can take, and your particular variables will alter the start-up cost. Rather than me giving you specific figures in this chapter, I will cover categories that you can apply to your given situation. This will help you determine a very rough estimate. The estimate is needed so you can figure out how much cash you need to gather.

When I say "start-up costs," I am referring to how much money it will take for you to get the doors open for business. Later in this chapter I will go over monthly operating expenses. Again, I am giving you a concise list, not an exhaustive one. You may find that, given your situation, there are other categories that would have to be added. This list is given with general childcare in mind. If you are interested in opening a special-needs center, there are going to be other categories not included.

Legal

You will have to hire a lawyer to draft your articles of incorporation, bylaws, stock setup (if you are a for-profit corporation), and other items.

Accountant

You will pay an accountant to work with your lawyer in reference to stock setup and to file for a tax ID number for your corporation.

Architect

You will employ an architect to draft all plans to be submitted to all agencies. You will be paying him or her to attend meetings with agencies and to work with your construction contractors.

Building

You will have to purchase or rent a building. There will be fees associated with your loan if you're purchasing, such as origination, appraisal, and survey fees. Some of these fees may be able to be worked into the loan. If you are renting or leasing, you will have a security deposit and have to work out the terms of construction cost as it pertains whether it will be the owner doing it or you. Typically, if the owner does it, the lease terms will be longer and its rate, higher.

Construction or remodeling items will include plumbing, fire alarms system, chiming system for all outside exit doors, heat sensors, smoke detectors, and so on.

Agency fees

You will have to spend money to have certain agencies review your plans and inspect your building. In addition, you will have fees for your licenses and permits.

Insurances

Some insurance policies you'll need include building, liability, auto, workman's comp, a daycare policy and others.

Furniture

You will need childcare furniture for all rooms, as well as office furniture.

Kitchen

You'll have to purchase commercial kitchen appliances. Your stove will have to have a commercial hood, your tri-compartment sink will need a grease trap, and you will need a heat sensor, as well as a smoke detector.

Educational equipment

Toys, tablets, bulletin boards, white boards, curriculum, and the like will need to be purchased. Based on your area, you'll have to have so many items per child enrolled.

Office equipment

Computers, a telephone system with an intercom, day care software, electric buzzer doors, and a camera system are all musts.

Advertisement

Be prepared to spend a substantial amount promoting your new center.

Vehicles

Start out purchasing at least two vans or buses. Purchase vehicles with a capacity for fifteen passengers or less. That way, your drivers won't need a commercial driver's license.

Tracking system

Each vehicle should have a tracking system, so you know where it is located at all times, as well as the speed it's traveling.

Where do I get the money?

Often, people will tell you get a good business plan together and go to a bank and try to borrow the money you need.

Or someone will recommend trying to get a small business association loan. Most of you reading this book know that your chances of getting a loan from a bank on your business plan alone are slim to none. Dealing with the SBA, you have a somewhat better chance. This is where most people get discouraged and a lot of times give up. As mentioned earlier, it's not about the amount of resources; it's about the amount of your resourcefulness.

Here are a few of the things I did in the beginning:

1. Used a $20,000 credit line from property we owned

2. Borrowed $10,000 from a friend

3. Maxed out every credit card I had

4. Got a friend to purchase a vehicle and paid the note myself

As you can see, in order to get resourceful, I had to give up my pride and ask for help. However, I had no problem asking for help because I believed in this 200 percent. As for the people I approached, even if they didn't believe in the project (as some admitted), they believed in me. I have always said, "I'll give up my dignity to get my deliverance any day."

Monthly operating cost

Below is a concise catalog of your monthly expenses:

1. Mortgage or rent

2. Utilities

3. Cell phones

4. Insurances

5. Alarm monitoring

6. Food

7. Vehicle notes

8. Vehicle maintenance/washing

9. Vehicle tracking

10. Gas

11. Office supplies

12. Payroll company

13. Building maintenance

14. Grounds keeping

15. Payroll

16. Classroom supplies

17. Cleaning supplies

18. Advertisement

Ideally you want to have three to six months of expenses in an emergency fund in some bank. I say ideally because, in the beginning, I had three months worth of backup, but the construction cost overran so much I had to use the emergency money to finish the job.

Control

One of the greatest financial lessons I've learned is that I am in control of the financial world of the business I run. I determine what money is spent on and how much is spent. I learned this principle: "Wealth is not how much you can buy; it's how much you can save."

At the time of this writing it is Thanksgiving Day. No, I didn't gather with family, eat turkey, and watch football all day. I have an objective and a deadline, so I am working during the whole Thanksgiving holiday. Like Les Brown said in a conference in Birmingham, Alabama, in 1998, "You must be willing to do what others won't do to have the things others won't have."

Tomorrow is "Black Friday." However stores now start their sales tonight. Tens of thousands of people are programmed to run out to stores and, in a lot of cases, spend money they don't have to spare to impress people who really don't care. It takes something called discipline not to follow the masses and opt for a better way. Discipline is what you'll need to steer the financial ship of your business. I define discipline as "forced obedience." You have to force yourself to do things in a certain way over a certain amount of time so it becomes a habit.

I work out five days a week. Some days I feel like it, and some days I don't. But I always work out. Since I've been doing this for years, I don't have a set time to work out. I just determine that, before I can go to bed at night, I have to work out. The days I don't really feel like it, I look in the mirror, and I love what I see. That motivates me to employ forced obedience so I can continue to see those results.

The same holds true with money management. If you want to see great results (a profit in your bank account), then you have to force yourself daily to control your money consistently and efficiently. You control your expenses and how you spend money.

I remember when the government used to pay providers once a month with a check. There were literally day cares that went out of business because they weren't disciplined enough to efficiently manage that lump sum of money for the whole month and make it last until they received their check the following month.

The biggest expense you are going to have is payroll. Payroll should never exceed 55 percent of your total operating income. In order to ensure that percentage, you will need to manage your time clock. Figure out who can be hired that can do more than one job. Determine when in the day you need full-time staff verses part-time staff. Never have staff sitting idly by doing nothing. At nap time, don't have too many people on the clock. Give your employees two-hour breaks.

Never be cheap in three areas

The following are three areas where you are never looking for a bargain.

Safety issues

Never cut corners with safety issues. Fix them quickly and hire the best. For example, don't run vehicles on tires that need to be replaced just to save a buck. Children's lives are in your hands.

Advertising

Never be cheap with any kind of advertising. Your advertisements represent you to the world. Henry Ford said, "A man who stops advertising to save money is like a man who stops a clock to save time."

Curriculum

Get the best curriculum for your children. The results from their learning will pay off in more ways than one.

Taxes

Never postpone paying your payroll taxes! You will have some tight financial times. All of us do. However, you are never helping yourself by borrowing your payroll tax money to meet current expenses. That's as bad as an employee of yours putting exempt on his or her W-4 form and saying, "I'll pay the taxes later."

Your accountant can put together a P&L statement for you so you can see where you need to improve. Always let your accountant do your corporate tax returns unless you are a CPA.

ACTION STEPS

1. Ask yourself, "Do I have a wealth mentality?"
2. Do you practice the wealth-building formula of spending less money than you earn?

3. Start determining your start-up costs and determine an approximate aggregate figure you will need in order to open your center.

4. Be resourceful and come up with ways to get the money you need.

CHAPTER 7

WOULD YOU GIVE UP YOUR DREAM HOUSE?

Expect the unexpected

Starting any business, let alone a childcare business, is hard work. I remember hearing a woman say, "I'm starting my own business so I can have more time with my family." I almost fell out of my chair laughing. If you have experience at entrepreneurial endeavors, you know that, in most cases, you will spend more time working for yourself than you will ever spend working for someone else—rightfully so. This is your baby!

Yes, I've worked for people and have been very loyal and dedicated. By nature, I am a hard worker and competitive. I'm the kid who got all A's in school (well except for in art and Spanish; I was crushed, but that's another story). No matter how hard I've worked for other people, it has never compared to the amount of time and energy I have worked for something I owned or felt I had a personal stake in. Currently I'm working fourteen-hour days. I have worked on Christmas and weekends. So, if you expect to be successful and do less work than you did when you worked for someone else, you are in for a rude awakening.

In elementary school, I was taught in science class that a rocket burns most its fuel not in space; rather, most of it is used on takeoff. It spends much of its fuel just trying to get off the ground and break away from what is holding it back—gravity. Expect to spend a great deal of energy and time just trying to get off the ground.

How long will it take for you to get off the ground? I don't know. In the beginning, it took three to four years before I saw strong returns. Now that I have expertise in what I'm doing, it takes me about two years, all things being equal. Along the way, several unexpected events will occur—unexpected simply because this is a new venture for you, and you don't have experience yet.

Curveballs are normal

Even for the most prepared individual, life has a way of throwing us curveballs. It's just part of the game. Personally, I think these curves are sometimes unique based on the pathway you are going down in life. While there are similarities between lives, I'm a firm believer that situations are heterogeneous because no one person is exactly the same as another. I've been through a lot of tough things in life. Some of these include:

1. A parent committing suicide

2. Temporarily being homeless

3. Walking two hours a day to get to the bus stop to catch a bus to work and having to carry groceries every day for two hours because I had no car

4. Being fired from a job at which I was the best in the conference for four consecutive years – If you added all the corporations up combined, they didn't come close to my production. My older boss didn't like my youthfulness (this was twenty years ago) and innovation.

I could go on. My point is this: These things made me who I am. While I don't like them and wouldn't want to repeat most of them, I am appreciative that I learned something from them. Even failures in my life have benefited me and a lot of times were the catalyst for the next success.

Michael V. Roberts, one of the most successful businessmen in America, wrote why he doesn't fear failure. He wrote, "Fear is a concept formed in your mind. It is not a physical impediment or barrier. Failure is only a representation of an unexpected or non-preferred outcome. This experience should merely be considered a learning event …as failure is only a mental enigma or aberration."[1] I am grateful for the learning; it wasn't always in the classroom though.

You are going to have challenges before you ever open the doors of your center, and after you open up your center. Don't look at these challenges as negatives; look at them as positives. Each time you solve an issue, you have now gained knowledge on how to solve that issue. When it comes up again, and I guarantee it will in some form, you will have the formula for solving that issue.

Some people believe that, once you make a certain amount of money, you never have financial challenges again. Well I hate to be the bearer of bad news, but do you plan on expanding and growing? I hope your answer is yes, because anything that is not growing is dying. If you don't plan on dying and do plan on growing, you will have financial challenges; they just won't be the same challenges. I have challenges today; only they come with a lot more zeros on their ends than they did eighteen years ago.

Architect numbers are off

Being naive, when I got the total cost of the project from my architect, I thought the numbers were ironclad gospel! I was excited that we had enough money and would have $3,000 left in our remodeling budget. Making a long story short, the project numbers were way, way, way, way off! I had to use my three-month emergency fund to finish the project. That was a huge blow, and we weren't even open yet.

Almost a year

All the agencies had approved our plans except one. This agency had our plans on its desk for almost a year before any review or inspection was done—almost a whole freaking year! Sorry. I'm having a flashback. Time kept going by, and I would occasionally call the agency. Finally, I started going to the agency's office to try to see what was taking so long.

Now I have my beliefs about why it took so long, but I will keep that to myself. I'll never forget what happened one Sunday evening. I was so agitated over nothing happening that I told someone who was close to me at the time that I was going to call the head of the department at home and cuss him out!

To this person's credit, she said, "Okay. But I doubt you cussing him out is going to endear him to wanting to help you."

I responded, "Maybe not, but it would make me feel a lot better!"

My friend replied, "Would that make you feel better or would getting the permission to open make you feel better?"

Well, I didn't cuss the department head.

Ironically, that Monday morning I got a call from the agency saying someone would be at my building at 2:00 p.m. if my architect could be there.

Twenty kids confirmed

Before our opening day, I had gotten parents I knew to commit to enrolling their kids in the new center. These were people I had known for years. I based my beginning budget off these kids and knew nothing but upward mobility was ahead, and we'd have a hundred kids in thirty days.

Opening day arrived, and only one child whose parents had promised would attend showed up. That's right, uno! I had hired staff for twenty kids, and now there was only one. What was I going to do?

Immediately I sent everyone on a two-hour lunch. Yes, a two-hour lunch at 7:00 a.m. I went into my office and designed some new color flyers quickly. I went to Kinko's, printed three thousand flyers, and headed back to the center. I sent teams of two to pass out these leaflets within a five-mile radius. They didn't have anything else to do; there were no kids.

You may be thinking, *What about the one child who was there?* Well, he was the son of one of my employees, so he rode in the car with her. With the three thousand leaflets, we got seventeen kids. I learned from this that you only get a .5 to 1 percent return on leaflets.

What are you willing to give up?

By this time, we had just started growing, but nowhere near quickly enough. I knew I was onto something with my concepts on childcare. Furthermore, something very interesting was happening. Childcare centers in my area were starting to go out of business as soon as I entered the market and changed the game. I am not implying that I put them out of business; I'm just noting the coincidence in timing.

However, I had some problems that I recognized were keeping me from getting over the hump to the land of profitability. Some of these problems were:

1. Free transportation was popular, but I was still in the experimental stage. Gas was costing us a fortune at the time.

2. Not enough people knew about my free transportation service incentive. Passing out leaflets was killing me. My youngest son, and I were the only ones passing out thousands of leaflets every Saturday.

3. It seemed that, as soon as I took children in, we lost children due to the parents getting kicked off the government subsidy program for some reason or another.

I realized I had to hit "critical mass" to offset the cost of the free transportation and have the concept truly working for me rather than against me in terms of cost. My advertising tactics weren't sufficient at the time.

One morning, I got an idea while driving the van to pick kids up from their homes. *The Steve Harvey Morning Show* was playing. My idea was this: "Advertise on the biggest, most far-reaching urban FM station in the area during the most popular show on that station."

As soon as I had that creative idea, a thought came into my mind: *You can't afford that expense.* Again, because I was naive at the time, I didn't realize the truth: It wasn't that I couldn't afford the advertisement; rather, I couldn't afford not to have the advertisement on that platform.

Not long after that, I remember hearing on some radio talk show someone saying that Henry Ford said, "Advertisement is never an expense. It's always an investment." Honestly, I don't know if Henry Ford ever said that or not. I took it as gospel from Henry Ford's lips, though. So, I determined it had to be done.

Then those negative voices started talking in my head again: *Okay, Mr. Determined, it's hard enough for you to just make payroll. How are you going to do this?*

I didn't have any free money, and I had already tapped out every person I could go to. Besides, this was going to cost multiple thousands of dollars. Then it hit me: What if I didn't have my house note and the expenses associated with it?

Now, you must understand this was my dream house. Prior to living there, I had lived in the adjacent neighborhood for about five years. Homes in that neighborhood were in the two thousand-square foot range. Every morning, I used to take my prayer walks, but I never went in my neighborhood; rather, I only walked in The Dominion. That subdivision had homes in the four thousand plus-square foot range. For five years, I used to tell my kids we were going to buy a house in that community. They used to look at me with the cynical look only a child can give and say, "Yeah right, Dad."

Well, one day five years later, it happened. I bought my dream home in that community. Everything about that home was fabulous, and whatever wasn't fabulous I made fabulous—from the Venetian plaster to the custom wood floors.

Now here I was after only having lived there four years, thinking about giving my dream home up. I knew that, with the given market at the time, I'd never sell it fast enough or for the price I wanted. I decided to let it be foreclosed on.

I started telling my friends about my decision, and they thought I had lost my mind. They didn't see what I saw. I knew this childcare center could be big. With my primary income stream drying up because of the Great Recession, to me it just made sense to put my money into a true asset that could grow, rather than continuing to put it toward something that was not a true asset. Robert Kiyosaki, author of *Rich Dad Poor Dad*, wrote in a recent article on his website, "Since the lesson still hasn't sunk in for many Americans, I'll repeat here: Your house is not an asset. It's a liability. Very simply, an asset is something that puts money in your pocket. A liability is something that takes money out of your pocket."[2]

In my case, this was true. The money I was putting into the house was bad debt because it was not putting any money in my pocket. If I put that money into the day care and used it for advertisement and expansion, then it had the potential of putting money in my pocket in the form of making sure I received a salary. It was a no-brainer to me.

The only person I had to convince was my youngest son, who was a teenager at that time—specifically, that it would be cool to live in an apartment. Well, when he found out his chores would be considerably fewer, he was totally on board.

I am, by no means, recommending that you do what I did. I simply am sharing my experience and allowing you draw your own conclusions.

The fact is, there will be a time when you must make a huge sacrifice in order for your childcare center to reach that next level. By me doing this, the center could reach critical mass, and it has never looked back. Either you are all in or you're not in at all.

Anyone who knows me knows I am a huge Alabama Crimson Tide football fan. I mean row two at the twenty yard line for the college football national championship in Phoenix, Arizona, when we beat the Clemson Tigers was one of the best games I have ever seen live. However, I am about to quote Dabo Swinnney, the Clemson Tigers coach. It's not heresy because football aficionados know he played for Alabama. Coach Swinney had a saying: "BYOG." Bring your own guts! If you truly want to win at this game of childcare, you are going to have to BYOG and make sure you have a lot!

ACTION STEPS

1. List good things you have learned that have come as a result of negative experiences.

2. Ask yourself, "What is the biggest sacrifice I am willing to make in order for my dream to come true?"

CHAPTER 8

BRAG PLEASE

Advertise

There is an old saying that goes something like, "If you build it, they will come." I've always had one question about that statement. How in the hell will they know where what you built is located? They won't—unless you advertise and tell them.

Usually the advertising budget is the smallest line item or nonexistent with childcare. There is this feeling that word of mouth alone will give a center major growth. That's only true if you have more than 350 kids enrolled. There is something about crossing that number that helps propel self-promotion.

Not long ago, I interviewed a woman to fill my directorship at a center. I asked her the standard question I ask all director candidates. What is your growth philosophy? She responded, "Well centers grow on word of mouth about the reputation of the director. Radio or television ads don't grow a center."

I leaned back in my chair and said, "Please turn around. Tell me, how many file folders do you think are on that table?"

She said, "I'd guess over a hundred."

I responded, "You are right, over a hundred. Those are new students just in the past two weeks because of our radio campaign."

Her philosophy was old-school and out-of-date, and the interview at that point was over.

Unfortunately, a lot of centers fail because they do not advertise properly. Be prepared to spend a lot of money on advertising both prior to opening and after you open.

You must become a great self-promotor. Forget all the things you've heard that tried to indict your character for daring to say you are good at something. Toot your own horn; toot it loud and toot it often!

Never forget

There is a key point that I never want you to forget: If you say you can do it, you better deliver!

You get one shot to impress people, so when they come into your doors, you better do it. If you fail, they are not only *not* coming back through your doors, they are going to tell ten or more people you really suck!

How much advertisement?

Henry Ford is quoted as saying, "Half my advertising is a waste. I just don't know which half." I agree totally with Ford. When I advertise, I spend to cast the widest net possible. One station I play my radio ads on is heard in three states, but I have only one center in that listening market. I realize a lot of people who hear my message won't need my service. However, enough people will hear it that do. I go this route because I always find my audience when I cast a wide net. Even reaching those who don't need my service is a benefit because, often, I've received calls from parents who say a friend heard the commercial and told me about you.

What kind of advertisement?

The kind of advertisement you'll want to use depends on the clientele you are going after. If my clients are primarily subsidized,

I don't spend a lot of money on web advertising. It just doesn't fit that demographic at the time. My best results have been to advertise on the largest, most popular urban radio station. If my clients are upper middle class, I advertise on satellite radio, the Internet, and talk radio. Your audience will determine how you advertise.

Leaflets

I don't do leaflets anymore. You only get a .5 to 1 percent return on distribution. If this is how you have to start, by all means, do so.

Radio

Absolutely. I advertise on the largest radio station based on my clientele's preferences. I only advertise during peak drive times.

Billboards

I will only advertise on stationary billboards. The new digitals have so many messages, and they switch constantly, reducing the likelihood of your potential client seeing your ad. Any billboards I invest in display only my advertisement all the time, or I don't spend the money.

Television

I'm not a big fan of television commercials now. However, I have some concepts I am thinking about trying to develop. There are so many stations, you have to practice saturation to get your message across, and that's very expense for a single center.

Internet

Yes, I do advertise on the Internet, as pertains to direct searches. Google's program is great. I am not a proponent of the old banner ads on any page.

Parent incentives

In the beginning, absolutely use parent incentives. Give your parents fifty dollars for every full-time child they refer and twenty-five dollars for every part-time child. After a certain point, discontinue this program. You just want to jump-start your enrollment this way. You don't want to program your parents to only refer when money is involved. You want them to refer you because of your outstanding service.

Teacher incentives

With the same amounts listed in the section on parent incentives, I always keep these incentives for teachers who work for me.

How to advertise

No matter what format you use to advertise, always produce high-quality advertisements. When using any print media, always use color and the best quality, brightest paper. If you are producing audio, always use a sound studio and the best engineer. Don't use your laptop and try to cut a commercial in your dining room. Quality always pays for itself and returns dividends.

When to advertise

Advertise all the time. A lot of providers make the mistake of trying to only advertise when they have available space. You want to constantly keep your name out in the public. While I understand you literally cannot afford to advertise every day when you get started, you do want to advertise at a minimum one week a month through a massive media format such as radio.

There are certain "hot times" in the year. During those times, I actually advertise every day for a month to six weeks during these times.

ACTION STEPS

1. Determine what forms of advertisement are best for your target audience.

2. Establish now that you will never make advertising an expense item. You will always look at advertisement as an investment.

CHAPTER 9

MIRACLES DO HAPPEN

What is a miracle?

When I say miracle, I'm not referring to the heavens opening, bright lights shining down, and your room being filled with angels. That would be a miracle though. If an angel is nine to twelve feet tall, you'd probably have a heart attack as well. No, when I say miracle, I'm referring to when God or the universe (whatever terminology you prefer) does something for you that you can't do for yourself, and everything just seems to come together.

A man named John

There was some property I was trying to sell to help fund us early on. The problem was that there were some repairs and other issues that had to be addressed before I could sell it. Furthermore, I was broke. It was going to take over $10,000 to fix and clear everything. Every place I tried to get money from said, "No!" I was discouraged and having problems motivating myself.

Someone once said, "If you cannot motivate yourself, then you are doomed to a life of mediocrity." The last thing I've ever wanted was to be mediocre.

I don't know where the thought came from, but I thought about a man who was a good friend of my father's. I always believed this man was a millionaire and so did many others, but he was very humble. Periodically, he and I had kept in touch over my childhood.

I called him and said, "John I need $10,000, and I will pay you back within thirty days. What kind of collateral do you need?"

The phone line was silent for a moment. Then John replied, "Collateral? You are Aaron Butler, Jr., right?"

I said, "Yes."

He said, "Dr. Aaron Butler's son?"

Again, I replied, "Yes."

John said, "You are like your father; I've seen it. If you give your word, you keep it. It will be there tomorrow."

Sure enough, the money was there the next day, and I paid him back early.

Subsequently, at a public gathering years later, John told the crowd I was one of the few men on the planet who could get anything I needed from him with a simple handshake. I never borrowed anything from him again, but I am appreciative that he was the vehicle of blessing he was in my life.

Tax refund

Money was tight, and we were honestly only making it week by week. I was doing my weekly cash flow one week and realized something. I didn't have enough money to meet payroll. Some money that was supposed to come in had not, and I was stuck like chuck. There was nobody I felt I could approach; either they didn't have it or I had already been to them, and my pride just wouldn't let me go back to them again.

Then I thought, *If my tax refund comes before payroll then, I can fund the shortfall myself.* When I got home that night, I went to the mailbox as usual, and there was a letter from the IRS. In short, the letter was saying that I would not be getting my refund, as someone else was claiming my son on her tax return as well.

Double whammy—I was short on payroll, and somebody was trying to claim my son, to whom I'd been the custodial parent since he was three, for a tax refund. I didn't know what to do.

So I prayed and asked God, not for the money but for what I call a "God idea." In my experience, the right idea brings in far more money than cash just to get out of a specific situation. Some of you may not believe in prayer. I promise, if you are about to become a childcare entrepreneur, you will learn how to pray.

This time, however, I didn't sense any kind of answer—nothing in my heart or in my head. I had two business days to turn in the payroll figures to our payroll company, or this was going to be the first time I'd missed a payroll. It was Saturday—my only day to sleep in—and something was urging me to get up. I didn't want to because Monday was going to be here before you know it, and I didn't have the payroll.

Finally, I got up and did my routine. I was sitting in the dining room eating a bowl of cereal when the mail carrier pulled up in her truck and put my mail in the box. After I ate, I went and watched some television. Something said, "Go get the mail." I internally rebuffed the notion, thinking about that old *Sanford and Son* episode when Lamont brings bills out of the mail and tells his father, who knows they are broke. Fred's response was classic: "Put them back in the box."

Finally, I said to myself "Might as well get this over with." I went to get the mail. As I got the mail, I noticed an envelope that was different from the others, with a cut-out open, and the letter looked golden. It was from the IRS and it was my refund. I was in shock. I wasn't supposed to be getting my refund according to the previous communication. I thought, *Maybe I should call the IRS.*

Then I said to myself, *Hell no! If they are wrong, as long as the check cashes, I can pay them back later.*

Now, I couldn't wait for Monday morning to arrive. I deposited the check, made payroll, and the IRS never contacted me about it; nor did I contact them.

Would $5,000 help?

Cost overruns were through the roof. It seemed that, with every day that went by, another expense would pop up out of the blue. Have you ever seemed to have something fixed on one end and then had it go haywire on another? That's exactly what was happening to me with this day care. It was one thing after another.

I remember the health department didn't like where a door was in a classroom, so we had to add another door. To make the job more difficult, that wall was made out of cinder block.

I could tell you story after story of changes regulators wanted—different than what had been approved. You can't argue, or the agency representatives may delay your opening out of vindictiveness. It's funny how some people with a little power act like they are Napoleon.

I wanted to quit, but I couldn't. I was too far into the project. I was facing a $3,000 shortfall, and honestly, I didn't feel like being resourceful. I was just getting numb. Yes, even driven and courageous people want to give up at times. I had made up my mind. I was done thinking about it, and I was going home.

I got up, grabbed my briefcase, and was about to head out when I heard a knock. I said to myself, *Great, I wonder what now.* I opened the door, and it was Big Red. Red said, "Can I talk to you for a second?"

I really didn't want to talk to anyone, and I could have brushed him off. But something said don't. "Come on in have a seat," I replied.

Red said, "I see you were about to leave. I won't hold you long. I was just wondering, would $5,000 help you?"

I looked at him, and I guess my facial expression said the question in my head, *Huh? Uh, why?*

Red said, "I know you've been struggling to make this day care happen. I believe it really is going to make a difference. So if five grand can help..." He pulled out $5,000 cash and laid it on my desk.

Okay, I was struggling, had a $3,000 shortfall, and there was $5,000 sitting on my desk. What do you think I did? I got up and gave Red a hug. He knew I always looked at him as a father figure, and I was truly touched, more than I can write.

I could tell you more actual accounts like these, where what I believe as divine intervention took place. I want you to see a pattern. Every time God or the universe moved on my behalf, it always occurred through a man or a woman. It's always going to happen through people.

This is why you can't cuss everyone out. Yes, you'll feel like it. And if you give in and do it, it'll sure feel good—at the moment. The problem is what if that's the person the universe needs to work through to get you your miracle? If you cussed the channel of your blessing out, how willing do you think he or she is going to be to help you?

Connecting the dots

Steve Jobs put it a different way in his 2005 commencement speech to the graduating class at Stanford: "Again, you can't connect the dots looking forward; you can only connect them looking backward. So you have to trust that the dots will somehow connect in the future. You have to trust in something—your gut, destiny, life, karma, whatever. This approach has never let me down, and it has made all the difference in my life."[1]

There have been so many times going forward when I didn't think things were going to get better. We all have those moments—the feeling that our moment is our eternity. When we're in the height of despair, we want to throw in the towel. If you truly believe in your vision to make a place where children are loved, taught and inspired don't give up. No matter the obstacles you may face, you will make it somehow and some way. Then you will look back and realize the greatest miracle isn't getting through the moment; rather, the greatest miracle is realizing you are not alone.

ACTION STEPS

1. List some times when God or the universe divinely worked on your behalf.

2. Look back over your life and recognize how the dots have connected.

3. Make this confession daily, "I am not alone. God, the universe, and spirits that love me are working with me and on my behalf, changing my circumstances."

CHAPTER 10

BEST IN YOUR WORLD

Unique you

Do you realize how special you are? Just like no two snowflakes are alike, no two human beings are identical. Molecular geneticist Shiva Singh of the University of Western Ontario found no two people are alike even if they are identical twins. He discovered this while studying the genetic determinants of schizophrenia.[1] There is such power in you being you. Haruki Murakami is quoted as saying, "So the fact that I'm me and no one else is one of my greatest assets. Emotional hurt is the price a person has to pay in order to be independent."

Too many times, we look at other people and wish we looked like them, acted like them, or possessed something they owned.

Ralph Waldo Emerson put it best when he said, "Insist on yourself; never imitate. Your own gift you can offer with the cumulative force of a whole life's cultivation, but of the adopted talent of another, you have only an extemporaneous, half possession." You never can be the best someone else. You can only be the best you because nobody is you but you. You don't have to be envious of anyone. You can have anything you see someone else have and more. Never sell yourself short by imitating someone else. Who knows? Maybe being you would allow you to get to where you see someone else faster and with a greater return. There is no one better than you!

A sense of urgency

Every day, I look at people living life like they have all the time in the world. They operate as if nothing special was happening. Something immensely special is happening right now. Time is going by as you read these pages—time you can never get back. These few moments you are reading these pages, you made the conscious choice to invest your time. Now with any investment, you want a good return.

My question to you is this: How well do you invest your time on a daily basis? What are your top objectives today? How do those overall objectives advance you to a goal you've set? What goals do you need to achieve in order for your vision to take place? Does your vision ensure you are operating in your purpose?

I threw a lot of questions at you there. Some you may understand, and with others, you may not have a clue what I meant. That means you should have a sense of urgency to know your purpose, develop your vision, set your goals and establish your daily actions.

You see, none of us know how much time we have on this earth. To my joy, I've seen people live over a hundred years in superb health. And to my sadness, I've seen children die at the tender age of three. We just don't know how long we're going to be here.

There is nothing you can do about how you've invested your time in the past. That is over and already recorded in the book of history. Yet you can do something about today and all your tomorrows. Make up your mind that you are no longer going to simply coast through life. Decide to live every moment on purpose and with no wasted motion. Determine that, during maybe the first quarter or even half of your life, you may have lollygagged away, but the rest of your life will not be the same.

There is a term that denotes a specific transition of time—BC. BC stands for "Before Christ." Why don't you today make a line in the sand and determine that everything from yesterday and before is your BC—not Before Christ; rather, your BC stands for "Before Consciousness." You are now conscious that every moment counts, and you have decided to live on purpose with a sense of urgency.

Your health

Now, if you are going to live life at your full potential, you are going to have to be healthy. Getting your childcare center off the ground is going to be a monumental task—and one I am sure you can do. However, you are going to need strength and energy to do so. About five and half years ago, I weighed 280 pounds, and I'm five eleven inches. That is big, people. I ate whatever I wanted whenever I wanted with no regard. I was always tired and sluggish. Since this is not a health book, I won't go into the intricate details, but today I'm 192 pounds, I eat right, I have great energy, and I work twelve to fourteen hour days six days per week. I've been this weight for over four years.

Take your health seriously. You can't be your best eating donuts and cake all the time. However, an occasional Krispy Kreme glazed donut on cheat day is permissible at 190 calories.

Go to the doctor regularly. Have all the tests and things done that pertain to your age. And follow your physician's directions. You don't want to do all this work and open a super successful day care have a heart attack and die. Then your husband takes your insurance money, sell the business, and goes on a round-the-world cruise with Becky, who now enjoys your money, your success, and your husband. Or after you've built a mega day care empire, you drop dead, and your wife is in the arms of some super muscle guy. Does that make you mad? Then go to the doctor!

Average why?

The news is filled with commentary about the "1 percent"—those who are doing so much better than the rest of us. The news never seems to focus on the amount of lazy people who just settle. I know you've seen these people. They complain about everyone and everything but never are willing to do the things necessary to advance their lives. These professional complainers have no problem being stuck on stop living average. Now the mere fact you are reading this book lets me know you are not one of them; they wouldn't dare pick up a book that would challenge them to do better.

Why have an average day care center? Some of you are thinking, *Because I have average or below average money at this time.*

You don't have to have money to be above average. Harold, my maintenance chief, has, for over twenty years, always worn jeans that are perfectly ironed, starched with a crease to perfection. Some of you are saying, "His wife is smart. That lets women know he's taken care of very well." You would be wrong in your assumption. Harold irons his own pants. Harold puts in a little extra time, which makes him stand out and be above average.

If you are willing to put in a little extra time in one given area of your center, you can be above average.

In the beginning, I decided my center would "exceed parent expectations." That is how I decided to be above average. So, we used to walk people from their cars with an umbrella of ours if it was raining or arrive before normal hours to accept a child. And of course the free transportation fits this as well.

With just a little extra effort, you can move from a C to a B.

You don't have to know everything

To be the best in your world, you don't have to know everything in the world. Having a lot of general knowledge about something amounts to just that—having a lot of general knowledge. You don't succeed by being all over the place. You succeed by being focused. In other words, you want specialized knowledge in a given area—in our context, childcare. Someone said, "I'd rather be known for doing something well than a whole lot of things loosely."

Concentrate on knowing everything you can about your type of day care. Become a master at what you do. Don't waste your time trying to know everything about business. If you do that, you will be like professional students who are always enrolled in a class and never get out in the real world and apply the knowledge.

Read, read, read

Be a vociferous reader! Read everything you can on the industry. Read everything you can on your community. Read everything you can about yourself as it pertains to human nature. Read biographies on successful entrepreneurs. Read articles on day care corporations. You cannot be the best and not be a reader.

Your world

I view day care like the universe—a wide expansive space with different worlds in it. Childcare provided by an employer on the company's property is a world, and low-income subsidized childcare is another world, to give a few examples. When you are striving to be the best, you aren't trying to be the best overall childcare. You just want to be the best in your world.

The two examples given earlier have vast differences and you cannot be all things to all people. Just because you see something working in one childcare center doesn't necessarily mean it will work in yours. One of the things we do at daycareman.com is be very specific about what kind of world the center we are working is in. Just like planets have different atmospheres and compositions, so do day cares. Focus on being the best in your world, not the best in the universe.

ACTION STEPS

1. Make a list of what is unique about you.
2. Access your current health state and, if needed, go to the doctor and make the necessary changes immediately.

CHAPTER 11

CLOSING TIME

Parents need you

The US Bureau of Labor Statistics projects that day care businesses will have some of the fastest employment growth of all industries through 2020.[1] The US Census Bureau figures show an increase to 766,401 childcare facilities in 2007 from 262,511 facilities in 1987.[2] Demand has been driven by increased numbers of working women according to the Census Bureau .[3]

Parents and soon-to-be parents need you to fulfill your dream of opening a childcare center. They need a partner who they can trust to help with the most precious commodity that exists—their children. They need you to persevere through every challenge and rejoice with every victory. They need you to open a center, fill it, and then open another and another and another—all with your high standards of excellence. Life is already tough enough for them. People already feel they are in this world alone. They need you to be it and do it.

Children need you

Frederick Douglass said, "It is easier to build strong children than to repair broken men." There are so many children that need to become a boy or girl of:

1. Character
2. Courage
3. Strength
4. Vision
5. Drive
6. Dedication
7. Love

When I was a child, I loved reading my comics. Two of my favorite comic heroes were Superman and Batman. Yes, you can imagine the movie *Batman v Superman* caused me some internal distress. Seriously, in my imagination, I believed Superman or Batman was always around to be my hero.

I remember being a child and visiting Washington, DC, for the very first time. When I walked in the Lincoln Memorial, I was awestruck. In my imagination, I believed that, if something happened to our country, Lincoln would rise off his chair and be our hero.

Children around this country and, as a matter of fact, around the world need a hero. They need you! You are that hero! You are the one who can provide a safe, clean, welcoming, loving environment they can come to every day. You are the one who, possibly, is giving them the best meals they will eat all week. You are the one who can teach them conflict resolution when two children want the same toy. You are the one who can teach them how to handle disappointment with grace when they aren't picked up at the time a parent promised. You are their hero. You deserve an "S" on your chest and a cape on your back for the heroic things you will accomplish through your day care.

Partners for life

These pages now link you and I together for life. I am always here to help you realize your dream. You can contact me 24-7 at daycareman.com and find out the services we offer to help you bring your childcare vision into reality. If you don't ever choose to visit the site, you will always have this book. These pages can be referred to over and over as a source of encouragement and inspiration. While time didn't permit me to go into more details on subjects like curriculum or buying an existing center and the many other topics that could be broached, my team is standing by to walk you through any and all stages of this most excellent journey.

Thank you

Let me take this time to thank you for giving your precious time to reading the musings of a day care junky. I am so excited about your future and thankful for the opportunity you afforded me to contribute to it in a small way. Be sure to get my free gift to you valued at $200 as another way for me to say thank you.

To Your Success,

Aaron Butler, Jr., aka the DAYCAREMAN ™

MY GIFT TO YOU

$200

To show my sincere appreciation for your having purchased and taken the time to read *Day Care DNA*, I am giving you a $200 coupon that can be used on any of the services offered at daycareman.com. Simply go to the website, follow the prompts, and receive your coupon. Together, we are going to make your day care dream a reality. Again, thank you.

AUTHOR BIOGRAPHY

Out-financed and out-resourced by all the competition, Aaron Butler, Jr., started Hope Academy Daycare & Preschool in the middle of the Great Recession. He has built one of the fastest-growing day care, preschool, and before- and after-school programs on the Gulf Coast. Inspired by two previous generations of educators, Aaron has introduced innovative concepts that have changed the lives of hundreds of children and their families. His education at Troy University and the University of South Alabama, coupled with his "street education," has aided him in developing a one-of-a-kind program that gets results. He is the president of Daycare DNA, Inc. A company that helps people start successful day care centers and helps existing providers create healthy and profitable centers.

Born in Michigan to Aaron Butler, Sr., BS, B.Th., MA, DD, JD, and Tommie Marie King Butler BA, M.S—two outstanding educators—Aaron now resides in Mobile, Alabama, and Orlando, Florida. Father, entrepreneur, senior pastor (semiretired), and author Aaron, Butler, Jr., has dedicated his life to making a positive difference in the lives of children.

Visit his website at daycareman.com

ENDNOTES

Introduction

1   Federal Interagency Forum on Child and Family Statistics, "Pop 1: Child Population," Child Stats.gov, https://www.childstats.gov/americaschildren/tables/pop1.asp.

2   ChildCare Aware of America, "What is the Cost of Child Care in Your State?" in *Parents and the High Cost of Child Care: 2016,* http://www.usa.childcareaware.org/advocacy-public-policy/resources/reports-and-research/costofcare/.

Chapter 1: How Are You Wired?

1   T. Harv Eker, *Secrets of the Millionaire Mind* (New York: HarperCollins, 2005), 75.

2   Paul Brown, "Franchisees Are Entrepreneurs (Let the Debate Begin)," *Fortune Magazine* (September 2012), http://www.forbes.com/sites/actiontrumpseverything/2012/09/19/franchisees-are-entrepreneurs-let-the-debate-begin/#1dac975068fd.

3   Jeff Eglin, "Entrepreneurs as Franchisees," *Entrepreneur*, January 2006.

Aaron Butler, Jr.

Chapter 2: Designing the Dream Team

1   Eker, Secrets, 85.

2   http://www.biography.com/people/thomas-edison-9284349#synopsis

3   Heather S. Duncan, "Economy Forcing Daycare Closures, Report Says," *The Telegraph*, July 2012.

4   Susan Chirs, "Hispanic Families Use Alternatives to Day Care, Study Finds," *New York Times*, April 1994.

Chapter 3: It's True: Location, Location, Location!

1   Jim Collins, Good To Great (New York: HarperCollins, 2001), 92.

Chapter 4: Build a Great Team

1   "Global Population Grew To 7.4 Billion in 2016, UN Report Finds, CBC News December 2016

2   Jim Collins, *Good to Great: Why Some Companies Make the Leap… and Others Don't* (New York: HarperCollins, 2001), 41.

3   Seth Godin, *The Dip: A Little Book That Teaches You When to Quit (and When to Stick)* (New York: Penguin Group, 2007), 18.

Chapter 5: Finding Your Niche

1   Paul Brown, "Entrepreneurs Are Calculated Risk Takers—The Word That Can Be the Difference between Failure and Success," *Fortune Magazine*, November 2013.

Chapter 7: Would You Give Up Your Dream Home?

1   Michael V. Roberts, Action Has No Season (Bloomington: Authorhouse, 2005, 2008), 118.

2   Robert Kiyosaki, "Repeat After Me: Your House Is Not An Asset," December 6, 2016, http://www.richdad.com/Resources/Rich-Dad-Financial-Education-Blog/August-2010/repeat-after-me-your-house-is-not-an-asset.aspx.

Chapter 9: Miracles Do Happen

1   Steve Jobs, "2005 Stanford Commencement Address," Stanford News, http://news.stanford.edu/2005/06/14/jobs-061505/.

Chapter 10: Best in Your World

1   United Press International, "Genetics of Schizophrenia Studied," UPI, http://www.upi.com/Science_News/2011/03/28/Genetics-of-schizophrenia-studied/UPI-58941301361007/?st_rec=20161301571417.

Chapter 11: Closing Time

1   Mary Ellen Biery, "Growth In US Daycare Businesses," Forbes Magazine, June 2014, http://www.forbes.com/sites/sageworks/2014/06/15/heres-the-growth-chart-on-day-care-businesses/#5469deb46405.

2   Ibid.

3   Ibid.

Made in the USA
Middletown, DE
07 April 2018